Gioachino
ROSSINI

IL BARBIERE DI SIVIGLIA
SINFONIA

Edited by

Clark McAlister

Study Score
Partitur

SERENISSIMA MUSIC, INC.

PREFACE

To be as popular as they are, the overtures to Rossini's operas have been treated very poorly by publishers, both Italian and foreign, throughout most of their histories. Even the most recent editions, as thorough as many of them are, do not answer all of the questions concerning textual matters.

It will probably always be so. First, many of the textual inconsistencies one finds come from Rossini's own manuscripts. During most of his career, Rossini was working at an incredibly fast and furious pace, so it is not surprising that some relatively small details would escape his attention. Also, working at such speed inevitably took a toll on the legibility of some of his manuscripts, thereby adding another layer of potential uncertainty. While the context will frequently clarify such matters, in numerous cases different readings are possible.

Second, these scores come from a time when performance practices still assumed that the written score would be modified in performance in certain fairly predictable ways. Broadly speaking, for example, a certain lightness of execution was expected, the notation of which in our own era requires a rather liberal use of staccato dots. In Rossini's time, this refinement of notation was not practiced.

Third, in the case of works written for the stage which were already frequently performed during the composer's lifetime, it is quite logical to believe that Rossini's manuscript scores represent only an intermediate stage in the perfection of his music. The world of opera, more than that of concert music, thrives on revisions and alterations. Many of these changes, of course, are made to suit specific circumstances, and the composer would not want them to become permanent. Norman Del Mar, in his invaluable book *Orchestra Variations*, points out that, on the other hand, some of these changes represent composer-sanctioned second thoughts and even, sometimes, improvements over the original version of the text to be found in the manuscript score. As Del Mar says, "Not all traditions are bad and many derive from the composer himself or the society to which he belonged."

The question, then, becomes how to distinguish one kind of change from the other—when a later source differs from an earlier one, which reading should be followed? If we accept that in many instances no definitive answer is possible, we must follow our best understanding of Rossini's style, both as an individual composer and as one working contentedly within the prevailing performance practices of his time. The present editions of these overtures seek to do just that—by examining as many sources as possible, to arrive at performing texts which both reflect the spirit of the composer and are as practical as possible for the use of modern orchestras.

There is one aspect of this and other scores of Rossini's that needs more clarification than will fit practically in the space of a footnote. One of Rossini's favorite string colors is the rhythmic tapping, or clicking, of the bow against the string, indicated by the instruction **battute**, or "beaten." Some writers (including Christine Amner in *The A to Z of Foreign Musical Terms* and Walter Kolneder in *Auffürungspraxis bei Vivaldi*) feel that this instruction at least implies execution by using the wood of the bow, col legno. But Norman Del Mar, in *A Companion to the Orchestra*, suggests otherwise. In his discussion of the term col legno he writes:

> It is true that if executed honestly with only the wood of the bow very little actual note is heard, and when composers write important note formations col legno, such Berlioz in the Witches' Sabbath movement of *Symphonie fantastique*, the players will generally cheat by turning the bows sideways to that a little of the hair also comes into play. If they cheat too much, only the hair being brought into contact with the strings, this creates a quite different device, which is found constantly in Rossini under the term battute. . . . None of these vertical techniques produces any enormous volume, especially in view of the cautious attitude of the musicians . . .

To this discussion, three further considerations may be added. First, it will be seen that this technique also yields a staccato "sound," so that the use of staccato dots in notating its use is unnecessary. Second, there are passages which lend themselves to this style of playing but for which Rossini did not indicate battute. When, in these editions, the editor suggests the use of this technique the term [battute] will appear, but the composer's staccato indications will be retained. Finally, Rossini is sometimes not clear about when players should return from battute to conventional arco, whether staccato or not. Although the context may seem to make these changeover points evident, in these editions battute will always be "cancelled" by the term arco.

Norman Del Mar, in his invaluable book *Orchestra Variations*, has given us a clear and precise summary of the textual history of the overture we know as that for *The Barber of Seville*. Briefly, this overture was first written in 1813 to precede *Aureliano in Palmira*, but was used again in 1815 for a different opera, *Elisabetta, regina d'Inghilterra*. The 1815 version differs from the earlier version in instrumentation, because Rossini had a larger orchestra to work with, and also in a host of details, which suggest that he had re-thought the music. The present edition of this overture follows the model of *Aureliano in Palmira*, but with the optional addition of parts for timpani and bass drum. Del Mar's discussion, published in 1981, confirms the assertion above that none of the existing editions can claim to be definitive, for the variousreasons given both by Del Mar and by this writer in the above discussion. Individual textual points, particularly those in which this edition departs from Rossini's score, are cited within the present score by means of footnotes.

I wish to thank Nancy M. Bradburd and Clinton F. Nieweg, Librarians (retired) of the Philadelphia Orchestra, for their insights and suggestions during the preparation of these editions. I am most fortunate to be able to partake of their vast experience in these matters.

The Editor
Spring 2006

ORCHESTRA

2 Flutes

2 Oboes

2 Clarinets (C, A)

Bassoon

2 Horns (E, G)

2 Trumpets (A)

Timpani (ad lib.)

Percussion (ad lib.)

Violins I

Violins II

Violas

Violoncellos

Double Basses

Duration: ca.7 minutes
Premiere: February 20, 1816 (with the opera premiere)
Rome, Teatro Argentina
Orchestra, Gioachino Rossini (conductor)

This study score is an unabridged reprint – in reduced format – of the large
conductor's score first issued in 2006 by E.F. Kalmus as A5640. The matching
large conductor score and complete set of orchestral parts are also now
available for sale from Serenissima Music, Inc.

IL BARBIERE DI SIVIGLIA
THE BARBER OF SEVILLE
Sinfonia

GIOACHINO ROSSINI
Practical Edition by Clark McAlister

42103

* Some recent editions reverse the rhythm in Vcl. and D.B. in this measure to match that of the Violins, but the result seems rhythmically unbalanced. That reading could result from Rossini's haste in preparing his manuscript, particularly considering that early manuscript parts show the reading given above.

4

* Here and in similar places, Rossini writes ♩♪, but compare with m. 37 and corresponding passages, where he writes ♩♪ for the same kind of figure.

6

* Violin 2, mm. 48-50 and 56-58, Rossini wrote [music notation], but the voicing shown is perhaps clearer, allowing Violin 1 in m. 48 and 56, and Viola in m. 50 and 58 to be heard more easily.

* Rossini is very inconsistent about the lenght of the note following the half-note in this phrase. Sometimes it is an eighth, as here, sometimes a dotted eighth. The eighth, with a sixteenth rest following, is perhaps more practical.

* Rossini writes *battute* here, but at this speed, the execution is doubtful. This edition substitutes ordinary *arco*, with staccato dots.
The Double Bass part has been similarly modified beginning at m. 123, and all three parts again at the corresponding passage later on.

42103

18

* Violin 2, Viola, mm. 225-228 and 238-241 -- Rossini slurs these parts ♪♪♪, but compare with Viola and Violoncello/Double Bass at 229-232 and 242-245.

www.ingramcontent.com/pod-product-compliance
Lightning Source LLC
Chambersburg PA
CBHW081155040426
42445CB00015B/1896